I JUST DID A THING

A Creative Approach to
PIVOTING
and Designing Revolutionary
Changes in Life and Business

PENNEY FOX

Published by LeNoble Publishing
First Edition, First Printing
ISBN: 978-1-955132-11-4

Contents

As a single footstep will not make a path on the earth, so a single thought will not make a pathway in the mind. To make a deep physical path, we walk again and again. To make a deep mental path, we must think over and over the kind of thoughts we wish to dominate our lives.

- Henry David Thoreau

CHAPTER ONE

The Power of Pivots

PIVOT - to make a fundamental change in direction

There are times in our lives when we find ourselves in need of a PIVOT. Something happens, forcing us to make a change in our business, our life or even our mindset.

When we were deep into the COVID crisis of 2020, I lost track of how many times I heard people talking about making a change or a PIVOT in their life.

Millions of people lost their jobs and found themselves needing to find ways to survive. They had to apply for unemployment and food stamps. They cleared out their savings to keep the lights on and pay their bills.

Their emotional stress and financial anxiety caused them to PIVOT. Perhaps they started a new business or maybe they went from a corporate job to working in an Amazon warehouse.

These are the moments where we look at our lives and know that if we don't start to view our situation differently, we're not going to make any big shifts to move past the situation. When we find ourselves living in Albert Einstein's quote, "Insanity is doing the same thing over and over again and expecting different results," knowing that new actions are required if we want to see different results.

I was not exempt from finding myself in a place to make a PIVOT when my business was directly affected by COVID. My main source of income is from private social media consulting programs with small business owners. Clients and I meet during a 90 day timeframe, and I walk them through everything from developing their content strategy to showing them how to be more effective with their time online and using social media to share their marketing messages.

When the pandemic hit, my work was certainly not considered essential. In fact, it was one of the first things business owners cut from their budget so they could pay their rent or keep their power on.

It became hard for me to respond to their objections about paying for my services when I knew that they were trying to figure out how to buy groceries that week.

Knowing these challenging times were directly affecting my social media consulting services, I made an intentional PIVOT in my business by focusing more on a subscription box product called **Create Your Business** that was initially set up as a side hustle to my core business.

I developed a hybrid self-coaching program that includes the delivery of a subscription box. This program was significantly lower cost than working with me one-to-one. Plus, the **Create Your Business** subscription boxes were delivered to doorsteps rather than a client trying to find the time to meet with me personally between video meetings and online school with their kids.

With the state of the economy at that time during COVID-affected economy before me, I made a PIVOT to move my focus to the sales of the **Create Your Business** subscription boxes rather than promoting my marketing consulting services.

When we talk about making a PIVOT, it's not only about your business and making money. A PIVOT is about making any fundamental change in a direction.

Think about those who lost their loved ones, or the ones whose lives have changed dramatically because of COVID.

Both women and men found themselves learning what life is like as a single parent dealing with everything from bedtime rituals to how to stay in their home because they were suddenly a one-income household.

But not all PIVOTs experienced are COVID-related. PIVOTS have been happening to millions of people way before we knew what the word coronavirus meant.

PIVOTS can happen when you're divorced from the person you thought you would grow old with. It can happen with the breakup of a long-term relationship when you realize this person wasn't who they portrayed themselves to be.

Or they happen when the woman who has spent 20 years being a stay-at-home mom is sending her youngest child off to college. It's time to PIVOT her life into an empty nester figuring out what she wants to do with her days that were normally filled with family-related activities.

Every one of us will at some point experience a PIVOT.

A PIVOT happens when we're tired of doing the same thing over and over and expecting different results.

A PIVOT happens when you know that pushing through the fear of change is greater than the pain of staying in the feeling of discomfort by not doing anything.

It's how we choose to move through the change that makes the difference and determines where we'll find ourselves when we come out on the other side.

Does the PIVOT happen inside or outside of us?

At first appearance, it looks like we make a PIVOT because things are happening outside of us like a loss of a job or getting a divorce from a partner who had an affair.

It would be easy to feel bad for ourselves; and cry or complain to anyone who will listen about how unfair life has been.

You know you can always find people who will feed into those emotions. They'll support your feelings of hurt and rejection by calling those who fired you or hurt you all sorts of horrible names.

But that would be admitting that life happens outside of you and not because of you.

That would be saying that you can't PIVOT until all those things and people outside of your control will do what you want, act like you want and talk to you the way you want.

When we only look to things outside of ourselves, we'll never be able to PIVOT effectively and move in any positive direction. And yeah, I get it - it's not that easy to just snap our fingers and change the way we think, feel and act.

Most of us spend about 80% of our day reacting to the stress in our lives. We think about the experiences, decide how we're going to feel - spending our day letting what's outside of us determine how we live.

We've trained our brains and our bodies to live in reactive survival mode to what's happening outside of us.

When you become aware that you're living by reacting, then you can decide to change the way you are thinking. You do have options on how you can respond. You have options like private counseling or working a 12-step program to sort through your internal processing.

Now I'm not saying that these things won't help you move through the process of making a PIVOT but also know, these options are once again, outside of you.

The 12-step program or the counselor will give you actionable steps to PIVOT but to really see those different results that you're looking for, you must want it from the inside. You must work a process to discover what's within; that's how you're going to keep moving forward to make the change you want.

What if there was something inside of you that you and only you could control?

Something that once you discovered its presence, you knew you could find an answer to help you make that PIVOT. Then once you do, you'd step into the life you've always wanted.

Before I tell you about that something that's inside of you, let me tell you about my good friend Debbie and what happened when she made a personal PIVOT.

Debbie has been participating in the Alcoholics Anonymous program for over eight years. She is so involved with AA that she leads local meetings and is a sponsor to many people in our community.

Through her years in AA, Debbie moved through the steps to train herself how to react to her outside world without using alcohol as her coping device.

She participated in every one of the 12 steps in the program to help her develop an inner sense of peace. She learned how to teach her brain to manage any outside stress without thinking she needed a drink to make herself feel better.

The changes she intentionally made within herself became apparent when she found herself in an angry interaction with her sister during a Christmas dinner at Debbie's house.

The argument was over something trivial and yet my friend couldn't shake the uncomfortable feelings within her about her disagreement with her sister. She later worked the AA program steps to help her identify the source of those feelings which then allowed her to move back into her peaceful state of mind.

But it was more than just the program and later an apology from her sister at play in this scenario. Debbie had spent years reprogramming her brain and body to react differently to what was happening outside of her. And when something came up that went against her now calm interior, her body and later her brain, sent her messages internally that this argument wasn't the norm.

We all deal with different pressures and problems outside our bodies but until we're able to make the significant changes inside of us, we'll never see the results that we're searching for.

The poet Henry David Thoreau said, "As a single footstep will not make a path on the earth, so a single thought will not make a pathway in the mind. To make a deep physical path, we walk again and again. To make a deep mental path, we must think over and over the kind of thoughts we wish to dominate our lives."

I want to teach you a process to learn how to use creativity to make that deep path within your brain to move you through your pivotal journey.

Let's talk about what's happening in your body and what that has to do with making a PIVOT

Throughout this book, I'll refer to scientific reasons why certain things happen as I show you how to use creativity to come out of your PIVOT stronger.

This lesson about what's happening in your brain is the first because it'll set the foundation for the groundwork that you'll use to make your PIVOT.

When it comes to your brain, there is no difference between the feeling of pure happiness or pure pain. Those emotions activate the same area of the brain called the Limbic System or the Emotional Brain.

This is that part of the brain that protects us from danger and pain; often referred to as flight or fight. When we find ourselves in a place of danger, the Limbic System kicks in to make our bodies either run to keep us safe or it puffs out our chests to encourage us to fight our way out of the situation.

The Limbic System isn't just for protection. It's the same place where we experience the feelings we get when we feel love or other warm and welcoming emotions. It's those strong emotions when we meet the person of our dreams, hold our baby for the first time after giving birth or play on the floor in a room full of puppies. It's that overwhelming feeling of pure love where it feels like our heart will burst open.

This part of the brain is pure emotion.

Located within the emotional brain is the hypothalamus that creates chemicals in the body called peptides. These peptides are connected to every thought and feeling, good and bad ones. The more intense your emotions, the more frequently the peptides are produced for those thoughts and feelings.

These peptides are then sent to the cells in the body thus explaining why when we feel emotions, we also feel a vibrational energy or a pain in a certain part of the body. For example, when someone gets their heart broken, they'll tell you that they feel a pain or a heaviness in their heart.

It's important to understand that peptides act like chemical addictions within our bodies looking for an exact match to every good or bad emotion that we are feeling. And your body has no preference over feeling the good peptides like love or happiness versus the bad peptides we feel with anger, fear or rejection.

Your body can't tell the difference between the good or the bad. The cells are simply looking for the addictive feelings of the peptides. The stronger the emotions, whether good or bad, the more your body craves the cycle of that chemical addiction.

The brain becomes conditioned to think these thoughts to create more peptides into the body. And it doesn't matter if the thoughts are positive or negative, the body is just looking to get its next hit of peptides.

So, knowing this, would you choose doing more of what feels good and makes you happy rather than thinking about the bad memories or the rejection from losing your job?

Understanding this is the starting point to how you're going to make a revolutionary PIVOT in your life. It's about making the choice to spend more of your time living in those happy moments and feelings. Of learning how to open the emotional brain to experience more feelings of happiness and learning how to create for the pure joy of creating.

Everyone reading this book has been brought to this place, to this moment to find your way through your PIVOT, to be the best you that you can be.

I encourage you to be open to a new way of thinking. I want you to breathe in all the positive possibilities and exhale all those negative beliefs you hold on to.

Be open to this journey as I guide you through new and different steps to more ways to feel good in your life through creativity. Be open to trusting the fact that the opportunities and ideas that come to you are your path forward to living the life that you've always wanted.

Using your creative energy to make a PIVOT means more than just wanting to make a change. It's about changing the way you deal with what's going on externally. And not to do it one time but to be consistent with these new behaviors so you can spend more time feeling joy.

Are you an artist? Of course you are.

Artists make change happen. Artists are humans who do generous work that might not work. Artists aren't limited to paint or museums.

You're an artist as soon as you announce you are. As a leader, a coach, a contributor, a designer, a musician, an impresario ... it's art if you let it be.

If you care enough.

- Seth Godin

CHAPTER TWO

We're All Born Creative

We all can be creative.

Think back to the time when your parents brought home a new TV or something else huge, like a new fridge in a great big box. While the thing in the box was super cool, you were eyeing that huge piece of cardboard that was tossed to the side.

And then for the next several hours or even days, you played with the box that the TV or some big appliance came in. Do you remember where your imagination went? Was it a castle or a boat?

Then ask yourself, "Why did you spend more time playing with that box instead of watching the new TV?"

Think back to those moments when you were a kid, and that box was more than just a piece of cardboard. You were using your imagination and being creative. No one had to teach you what to do with that cardboard, you just knew what would happen when you got out the markers and a pair of scissors.

I am asking you to believe that you can be creative, even if the last time you picked up a crayon was when you were five years old.

As you move through each chapter and do the creative exercises, you'll uncover something deep inside you, something you might not have felt since you were that little kid playing with a cardboard box.

The creative exercises at the end of each chapter are designed to show you how to spend more time in the happy emotional space of the brain and to train your thoughts to deliver more of those good peptides into your body.

A few things to know about the Creative Exercises

The biggest thing you need to know about the PIVOT creative exercises is that what you think matters. I mean that quite literally - when you learn how to think differently, you'll start to up level what's going on within your body which will lead you to make more impactful changes in your life.

The other important piece to use creativity as part of your PIVOT strategy proposed in this book is that you don't need a checklist of things to believe in. You need a plan to practice bringing more of the good creative energy into your body.

As you work through your own personal plan of action, I want you to do the following:

1. **Commit to paying attention to how your body feels.** Those good feelings of joy and excitement are your body's way of telling you that you're moving in the right direction. And when your body feels anxious or there's a strong feeling somewhere in your body, take a step back and assess the choices that you're making.

    Just know that it'll take time before your body gets accustomed to this new way of working through your changes; so be patient with yourself if you slide back to your old patterns and ways of thinking.

2. **Commit to having fun with the process.** Go into this with an open mind to new ways of thinking and knowing that the consistent practice of making these changes is going to reinforce the shifts you'll continue to see.

    Staying consistent doesn't mean doing the same thing at the same hour or same minute of every day. It could mean doing your steps always in the morning or right after you come home, and your child is doing their homework. It's being mindful in the present moment – each moment – to know what works for you.

3. **Commit to giving everything a try.** Suspend your judgement about a certain step or part of the process. That's mindfulness in practice. Most people will read something and say, "Oh, that's not me. I can't do something like that." Rather than take that negative mindset, try it out.

Even if it's a smaller version of the idea, before you decide that you can't add this to your daily routine – try it. Sometimes when we take a couple of steps outside our comfort box, we realize it's not so bad out there. And there's no better feeling than to accomplish something that we thought we could never do.

Sharing my creative story

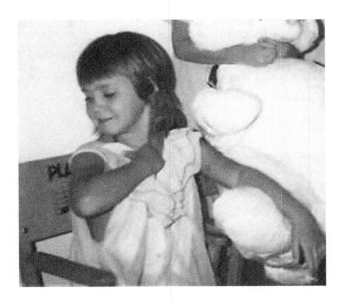

See that little girl? That was me at about the age of six in my childhood bedroom.

I didn't have a lot of kids in my neighborhood to play with at that time. It was primarily me and my older sister.

And my imagination.

11

When you spend a lot of time by yourself as a child, it's easy to spend time with your imaginary friends traveling to places that you create in your head.

Looking back to my childhood, I realize that we had quite a lot of creative energy flowing in our home. Both my mom and sister played the piano and later my sister learned how to play the clarinet.

When I reached an age deemed old enough to dig into my own musical talents, my mom asked me if there was a particular instrument that I was interested in learning. Without hesitation I said, "The drums! I want to learn how to play the drums."

As a parent now, I can certainly understand her concerns with my enthusiastic response. She was thinking about the noise drums would make in our small two-bedroom apartment. My mother's response as she shook her head was, "How about we sign you up for art classes?"

And thus began my love of creating art.

I took any art class or program in my community to keep feeding my desire to create art projects. By the time I reached high school, art class was my standard for my elective classes, and I moved past the ordinary drawing of a fruit basket.

I've always had a big imagination. In one of my art classes, I painted a picture of a pineapple car.

See the picture below of my high school masterpiece.

It is a framed piece of art that still hangs in my mother's home.

During those younger days, I would have never called myself an artist or even creative for that matter. I didn't see my future as someone who would make art for a living. I didn't even know why I was drawn to wanting to paint or draw pictures of cars made of fruit.

I created for the pure honest sake of moving through the process of creating.

I certainly wouldn't have called myself an artist when I took art classes in my 20s that coincided with pursuing my second college degree in the Visual Arts. Nor would I have considered myself creative during the time I tried to write a kids' book in my 30s.

I have a business degree and have spent most of my adult life working in marketing. I couldn't see how someone who was a marketing consultant could be qualified to call themselves a creative. I always connected that term with someone who made their living selling their art.

I didn't look at myself in a creative way until I found myself developing the **Creative Insight Process** as the foundation of my self-coaching product - the **Create Your Business** subscription box. The process developed from one of my core ideas that business owners need unstructured play time to help them build their business.

For the past 20 years I've coached women in various stages of owning their small business. From all those years of working with women with an entrepreneurial spirit, I designed the **Creative Insight Process** to give them the tools to activate the creative side of their brain.

I subscribe to the theory that we are all born creative. We just need to learn a path to help bring the creative energy out of us and into our lives.

And creative energy doesn't always mean that you're painting or drawing. Being creative could mean cooking a new recipe or planting a rose garden. It's more about being active with your body and the thoughts in your brain rather than sitting at your computer scrolling through Facebook.

If this concept is new to you, you may be struggling to figure out how being creative is going to help you make this PIVOT. You're having a hard time understanding the idea behind the **Creative Insight Process** because your brain hates the idea of thinking differently.

You're predisposed to doing the same things over and over, whether it's working or not.

And because we find ourselves doing the same thing, we tell ourselves that this will be the time that something different will happen. But we continue to find ourselves staying in the same place year after year.

I get it - it's not your fault.

You haven't been shown another way to turn your idea into a real income-producing business or to move past the hurt of a decades' long relationship.

I know that there's a ton of advice in blog posts and YouTube videos to help you make a shift in your life, but unfortunately, the information doesn't seem to go beyond the recommendations that "you've got to work harder" or "just believe that you can do it."

This whole PIVOT process is messed up, not you.

I want to give you the opportunity to set yourself free by navigating your new direction in a totally creative way to see real change in your life.

GET OUT OF YOUR BOX CREATIVE EXERCISE #1: YOUR CHILDHOOD BEDROOM

If you want to start changing the default setting in your brain, you must start making changes to replace the bad peptides that we talked about in the first chapter. One of the best places to start seeing those shifts is to use your imagination and go back to those times when playing with a cardboard box was the best thing in the world ever.

Due to something in your body called neuroplasticity, your brain can carve out new paths to create a more positive pathway. The pathways that are used more frequently and reinforced are the ones that become habits.

Each of the creative exercises that you'll experience will give you a new technique to help you find those pathways to your natural state of creative joy that you experienced as a child.

Creative Tools needed:
- Notebook and your favorite pen OR a Word Document on your computer
- Timer on your phone or on your computer
- Quiet place for 30 minutes

Think about your childhood bedroom. Remember the colors in the room, your toys, the furniture. What could you see when you looked out the window?

Get out a notebook or pull up a Word document to make some notes about the details that you remember about your bedroom.

Now, think about one thing that you remember and what it meant to you? Set the timer for five minutes and write your responses until the timer goes off.

If you're feeling the creative energy coming up inside you, I encourage you to go with it, grab some crayons and a piece of paper to draw something from your memory. It could be the layout of your room or something you remember hanging on your wall or even a favorite toy that always sat on your bed.

After each creative exercise that you work through, I want you to do a Get Out of Your Box check-in with where you are in the creativity process.

Questions to use after the creative exercises:

4. What did I learn about myself after doing the Childhood Bedroom exercise?

_____

_____

_____

_____

_____

_____

5. What did it show me about what happens with my thoughts when I'm adding more creative energy in my life?

_____

_____

_____

_____

_____

6. I am excited about _____

7. I'm proud that I did _____

8. What did you create after doing the creative exercise? This could be something you created when you got out those crayons or something that you ended up making a few days later.

_____

_____

_____

_____

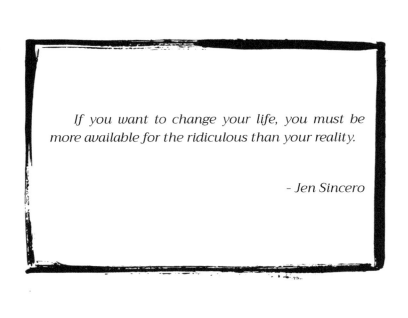

If you want to change your life, you must be more available for the ridiculous than your reality.

- Jen Sincero

CHAPTER THREE

A Tale of Two Pivots

Meet Annie and Carol. Two women who found themselves experiencing a PIVOT in their lives and who decided to move through the changes by opening themselves up to their own creative energy.

Annie worked in the marketing department of a large company in the Charlotte, NC area. For about a decade she served as the Marketing Coordinator for their clients and over the years, with several promotions, obtained the position of Director of Strategic Projects.

Annie loved working with her company's clients and watching their businesses grow from the marketing projects she managed. Everything was wonderful until COVID hit her area.

When they were sent home to work virtually, Annie became an expert at Zoom calls. Two months into the pandemic, her company cut her hours. By month number four, everyone in Annie's marketing department was let go without any indication if the job suspension was temporary or permanent.

Annie was devastated. Still, the severance package was more than enough to keep her afloat for at least six months. She also had money in savings and her 401K, so she didn't feel any immediate financial stress.

But she knew that her money would only take her through the holidays, so she needed to find another source of income. She started the work of finding a new job.

But no one was hiring, and depression became a part of her daily routine. Some days, it was hard to get out of bed and face another day full of rejection. It was exhausting; but every day, she forced herself to find the time to sit at her computer and look for any opportunity.

One day while connecting with some of her old clients on LinkedIn, she got an offer to work on a small marketing project. It was less than half of the hourly rate her former position paid but it was work.

And it felt good to have purpose again. That small job led to three more offers from other former clients. Annie realized that she could offer her skills as a marketing consultant to other small businesses.

Annie had spent enough time working on marketing strategy and knew what she needed to do to start getting more marketing clients. She had to do something that would stand out and get their attention while showing them how creative she could be managing their marketing projects.

She came up with an idea to send her past clients a monthly package with some cool office supplies or a business book. In each one of her packages, she added a postcard with a quote or a beautiful image that the client could hang in their office. On the back of the postcard, she included her latest marketing package and her contact information; in case they were ready to bring her on to help with their marketing plans.

Even with her extensive marketing background, Annie never considered herself to be a graphic designer, but she wanted her potential clients to be impressed with what they received. She understood the basics but hadn't really done any designing herself. She found an online graphic printing company that gave her several templates she could use to create the marketing package postcards. Then she would hit publish, the company would print the postcards and mail them to her.

It was an easy process, but what really grabbed her attention was how much fun it was to design the postcards. Finding the images made her dream about places to visit. Looking for quotes to use helped her think about how much she was enjoying being her own boss.

She grew to love the design process of adding in diverse colors and fonts and arranging the images to create her marketing postcards. It was like watching her messages visually come to life. Making the marketing postcards became one of her favorite things to do in her week.

During these design sessions, Annie noticed that her depression would lift, and she looked forward to the times when she could create for the pure sake of creating. She was excited again and even enjoyed taking her marketing packages to the UPS store to mail them out.

And what happened during those hours when Annie focused on designing her postcards? She began the process of retraining her brain to move out of depression and anxiety around her income to feeling confident that she could be successful as a marketing consultant.

What happened with Carol and her PIVOT?

Carol's life was completely different from Annie.

Carol was married to her high school sweetheart and together they raised three kids in a small town in California. Her husband had an amazing job as a managing partner in an investment company which allowed Carol to stay home with their kids.

One of her favorite things about being a stay-at-home mom meant that she was able to attend all her kids' activities. From being a baseball mom to her youngest son to organizing the pre-prom party for both of her daughters and their friends. For the last 28 years of her life, Carol spent her days and many nights taking care of her husband, her kids and managing their schedules with the ease of a highly organized event planner.

Her days were happily filled, and she felt the daily gratitude from her family. Until that fateful Fall came, and her youngest son went off to a college that was a five-hour drive away from home. Her other two daughters had already started their college journey and one was even in graduate school to become a teacher. Carol was sad to see her girls leave but when she dropped her son off at his freshman dorm, a feeling of anxiety came over her on the long drive back home.

Carol came home to an empty house.

She knew her husband would be home later that night from his job but that didn't help stop the knots moving around inside her stomach. It was like her motor was running and every time she thought about all three of the kids not being home, her internal engine revved up.

Her thoughts were creating more anxiety which just upped the intensity of the energy circling inside of her.

Carol spent the next two weeks after dropping off her son desperately trying to soothe her feelings. She went for walks in her small town. She tried to find a program to binge watch on Netflix but discovered that these were just distractions and her internal motor continued running. By week number three, she shared her concerns with her husband, and he suggested that she think about the time like early retirement and find someplace to volunteer.

It was a great idea, but Carol had never worked a day in her life. She married her husband right after high school and within the first year of their marriage, she was pregnant with their first daughter.

She was 48 years old without any work experience. How was she going to have an early retirement when there was nothing to retire from?

A month into her continuing to feel her internal vibrational energy, Carol was in the kitchen baking a birthday cake for one of her neighbors. She had always enjoyed baking, especially during the days when she volunteered to run the bake sales to raise money for the baseball team.

With her hands deep in the flour and all her ingredients spread out on the kitchen island, a thought hit her. How much flour and ingredients would it take to make 20 small cakes? She quickly did the math in her head and looked around her pantry to see if she had enough of all the ingredients. Indeed, she did.

After completing her neighbor's birthday cake, Carol got out the supplies needed to make 20 small little two-layer rectangle cakes with buttercream frosting. She wasn't sure why she needed to make 20 little cakes, but she noticed that for the first time in a month, the consistent feeling of the energy in her stomach was decreasing. So, she kept on baking.

After she put all the cakes into the oven to bake, a thought came to her about a small art boutique she had seen on one of her many walks into town. The shop featured art from locals as well as some other products like handmade soaps and honey from people in her community. Carol decided she would take her cakes down to the shop and see if they would sell them.

She wrapped up the cakes in clear cellophane, tied a big red and white checkered ribbon on each one of them and put them all into a big basket. Carol walked into that store with an idea and a basket full of cakes and walked out as the newest vendor in the art boutique.

Over the next few weeks, the anxious feeling in Carol's body went from a low grade level to non-existent. And when her kids all came home from college for the holidays, Carol was busy filling orders for the store and for special orders for a wedding and a 50th birthday party.

She was thrilled to see them come home but when they went back to their lives, Carol was no longer filled with anxiety or sadness. She found her happiness in making her cakes. She used her creative energy to override those bad feelings and found her next big adventure in her life as a baker.

Postcards and Cakes

One of the greatest things that you have to help you through your big change is your imagination.

With your imagination, you're not relying on your physical environment or someone else to do something for you. Spending time in your daydreams will give you everything that your heart and mind desire from your life.

A big part of using the **Creative Insight Process** as the process for your PIVOT is to use your imagination to push yourself out of your comfort box. When you spend time living in your daydreams and not in your current reality, you're able to play out all the possibilities that your mind can come up with.

I want you to start thinking big.

I want you to allow the ideas that come to you to be up for consideration before you quickly throw them away because you don't have the money, the education, the skills or whatever you think you need to make that dream come true.

Because when that big idea comes up in this process that feels so huge and out of your reach, that is exactly the point when you need to really believe in its possibility to turn your dream into a reality.

GET OUT OF YOUR BOX CREATIVE EXERCISE #2: ALL THE MONEY YOU NEED

This creative exercise is going to show you how to spend more time using your imagination. Spend more time being deliberate in your daydreams, not just those moments when you catch yourself staring into space.

It's more like that story about the Rocks and the Jar that teaches us how to prioritize our time. We've all heard one of the many versions of this story. Teachers, speakers and CEOs share it in lectures and meetings often.

The speaker takes out a large jar and fills it with big rocks. Is it full yet? Yes, everyone says.

Then he adds small pebbles, asks the same question and awaits responses. From there he adds in sand, asks his questions one more time before driving home his point by pouring water into the space left in that great big jar.

The moral of the story is to always put your big stones/projects on your calendar first so you can find time to work on them or you'll fill your day/jar with every little thing { busy work }. Then you'll never find the time to work on those big important projects you want to accomplish in your life or business.

But what if we use the last step in that Rocks and Jar story as a form of dreaming?

How can we work to our full potential every day if all we're doing is filling our jar with big rocks, little ones and all that busy work from the sand?

What if we were able to find more ways to add the water into our jar to dream about the changes we want to make in our lives?

Creative Tools needed:
- Notebook with you favorite pen or Google Document on your computer
- Timer either on your phone or on your computer
- Quiet place for 30 minutes

Think about the following statement: If you had all the money you needed, what would you do with your day?

Set your timer for 15 minutes and start writing or typing your answers. Let there be no judgement about what comes up regarding money or the skills involved in what you would do.

Imagine yourself in your new activities. What are you doing? Are there other people there? Where are you located? What conversations are going on? Keep writing until you reach the full 15 minutes of time.

Then set another 15 minutes on your timer and document any ideas that came up as you were using your imagination. Did you get an idea that's connected to your PIVOT? Use the 15 minutes to build on your insights and see what kind of plan unfolds that you can start to implement.

If you're feeling the creative energy coming up inside you, I will always encourage you to go with that feeling by doing the following creative project.

Get out your cell phone and look at the last 10 photos that you've taken. Use an online photo editing app like Snapseed, Pixlr or A Color Story and add in some filters and effects to one of your photos. Spend some time using your imagination to add something fun that you normally wouldn't include in a social media post.

After you've spent a little time playing with the editing app on your phone, I want you to do a Get Out of Your Box check-in with where you are in the creativity process.

Questions to use after the creative exercises:

1. What did I learn about myself after doing the All the Money You Need exercise?

2. What did it show me about what happens with my thoughts when I'm adding more creative energy in my life?

3. I am excited about _____

4. I'm proud that I did _____

5. What did you create after doing the creative exercise? This could be something you created when you edited your photo or something that you ended up making a few days later.

We can't solve problems by using the same kind of thinking we used when we created them.

- Albert Einstein

CHAPTER FOUR

How Einstein Can Help You

We all know about all the amazing things that Albert Einstein discovered in his lifetime. But everything wasn't always uncovered with brilliant ease. Einstein had several moments when he was struggling or stuck trying to determine how to move forward.

And when he was in this place, he would shift his attention to what he called "combinatory play." Combinatory play is the act of rejuvenating the analytical part of the brain by participating in something that opens the right side of the limbic brain or the creative part of our thinking.

Einstein learned to play the violin.

When he was struggling with solving a math problem, he would spend hours playing music until the answer appeared as an insight. Einstein's version of combinatory play is what I call the **Creative Insight Process**. This is the process that will teach you to spend more time in the creative side of your brain.

Now that you've learned about the basic science of what happens to your body, I'm going to break down how you're going to use the **Creative Insight Process** to make that big shift in your life.

I often tell my social media consulting clients that when they get stuck, when they find themselves struggling with what to do next, do something creative. It can be something as simple as walking your dog and noticing the colors on the leaves of the trees. Go paint a picture or paint the walls in the downstairs bathroom. Bake a cake for your family.

{ As you keep reading the words 'do something creative' please remember these examples - being creative doesn't always mean painting or making a craft project. It means doing something physically different that takes you out of your normal routine. }

It doesn't matter what you decide to do, just don't sit there feeling overwhelmed ... do something.

Some of you may be thinking – but aren't I just ignoring my problem? Am I just procrastinating and taking my focus off what I'm trying to accomplish?

Yes. You are shifting your focus by tapping into the **Creative Insight Process** just like Einstein did when he picked up his violin.

But you're not ignoring your problems. It means you're choosing to act differently. Any action beats feeling the struggle.

And any action using your creative energy – no matter what it is – will draw out your inspiration and help you uncover the answers that are eluding you.

Insight is Creativity

Before I take you through the steps of how the **Creative Insight Process** works, know that this information has NOT come to me because I'm a scientist, counselor or a doctor.

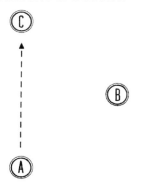

I'm telling you about this process because I saw the shifts happen in my life that helped me make my own big PIVOT.

I saw it happening to others around me, but we could never put a name to the thing that was happening. I would find myself going from Point A to Point C { creativity } but I was never quite sure what happened at Point B and how I got there.

I started researching and found the names to the why and explanation to the how.

What you are experiencing is my journey to change the direction of my life by opening myself up to my creative energy.

This is the story of how I discovered how the dots got connected.

How the Creative Insight Process disrupts your Prefrontal Cortex

The prefrontal cortex is that part of the brain located in the front behind our foreheads. Its main function is to take the messages received from different regions in our brain and body and process this information. The prefrontal cortex is developed to help you act on things like planning, decision-making, problem-solving and self-control.

When you're having a conversation with someone, this part of the brain allows you to focus on what she's saying and then manages your emotional reactions while allowing you to decide on how you'll respond.

Our brains are highly developed to operate efficiently using a neural pathway to help you reach a goal. When we do an action repeatedly, the prefrontal cortex creates the neuropath to allow us to do these actions without even having to think about the specific actions involved.

Think about the actions you do daily like brush your teeth or put your pants on. You don't think about which leg goes in first or which area the toothbrush goes to when it first makes contact in your mouth. You just do the behavior.

The more times that you repeat these behaviors, the actions become embedded into your brain and become a habit. And after a significant amount of time, these habits become automatic. We no longer think about what we need to do to make our bodies react.

We go into autopilot.

How many times have you driven home from work or the grocery store and don't remember how you got home? You've driven that route so many times that you've trained your body to do the right turns and the exact steps to get back to your house without your brain having to tell it to do anything except to stop at that light.

For you to experience the **Creative Insight Process**, you'll need to learn how to disrupt the autopilot mode in your prefrontal cortex. You may call this a distraction but to learn how to retrain your habits, you need to be adaptable when these moments arise rather than remaining in the state of autopilot.

Several studies regarding making a shift in creative energy have shown that the attention provided to the act of doing something creative greatly affects your thoughts and behaviors. When we disrupt the information moving through our prefrontal cortex by actively participating in acts of the creative process, we allow new thoughts and habits to flow.

And for you to truly make that PIVOT in the direction of your life, you need to replace the old habits that make you feel anxious. You need to shift those old thoughts that make you feel stressed into something that's going to help you make necessary changes.

You need to treat your thoughts like they are a Statue of Liberty snow globe. Shake that thing up as hard as you can and then watch the snow swirl around, fall to the bottom and away from Lady Liberty.

Let me show you how this works

Like many other business owners, my consulting business was devastated during 2020. In my more than 22 years of working for myself, I never had conversations with potential clients as I did that year.

I've learned over the years to deal with questions about why someone would want to pay for my consulting services. I'd launch into a detailed explanation of telling them how much time they'll save tapping into my many years of marketing experience. How much clarity they'll uncover when we spend three months focusing on their marketing strategy and they'll have a plan in place to implement their social media strategy.

But the objection of "I can't pay you because I need to keep the power on or buy groceries this week," well that one, that's hard, if not impossible to dispute. There's no marketing experience or counterpoint that could possibly replace the fact they needed to hold on to whatever money they had in their bank accounts to eat, live and provide for their families.

Within two months after America went into the pandemic lockdown, I had zero clients and was working my way through my savings account. I had also launched the **Create Your Business** subscription boxes and with money and time invested in that business, I decided to push on without knowing if I could make it my primary source of income if my consulting business failed.

Another month in, I found myself treading water trying to keep my own power on and asking for money from my parents and friends to get groceries for the week and pay the bills.

I felt myself falling down a financial well without a plan to crawl my way back out of it. The emotional stress of dealing with financial stability can sure take a toll on a person's mind, body, and spirit.

When I realized that my usual way of managing my business wasn't going to work, something inside of me knew that it was time to disrupt the autopilot steps I kept trying to force myself to follow. The words prefrontal cortex never entered my thoughts, but I knew there was another way.

With my financial mess screaming in my face, all I could do during those moments was to close my eyes, breathe and create art. I found my old paintbrushes and some art supplies left over from the **Create Your Business** boxes. I started to paint again.

I knew it was a distraction, but my body and brain were desperately looking for another outlet for my attention.

Did I really need to think about my problems all day? No, I didn't.

That thought alone led me to think about what my day would be like if I found two hours where I could intentionally not worry and do something that made me happy.

And what happened during those hours when I focused on my art projects? I retrained my body to shift from feeling that anxious stress to thinking about something cool that I could do to help promote the **Create Your Business** subscription boxes.

I painted and the idea came to me to do an interactive workshop with my community to have them do something ... maybe they could paint with me? Well, that would be hard for people who were showing up to learn about social media marketing.

I cleaned my brushes and moved on to the next layer of paint. What if I gave them some creative exercises in between the learning sessions? Something that they didn't have to buy art tools to do but something where they could use their imagination.

Insights and ideas started to flow to me so quickly, I stopped and grabbed a pen to scribble notes on a scrap piece of paper.

And it didn't just happen that one time. It has happened to me EVERY time I work on one of my art projects. I settle into the creative experience with a question in my mind and usually during the creative project or later that day, a solution will come.

Knowing this is going to happen makes me want to find more time to create. The actions of getting out my brushes and a new canvas will trigger my brain to know what's coming.

I've created a habit that adds moments of happiness which allow new opportunities to enter my thoughts.

This new habit has affected my behavior which then produces new emotional peptides in my limbic brain. And when I do these habits consistently, it creates a new experience that replaces the anxiety and stress with positive emotions and allows me to find a new way to make my PIVOT and grow my subscription box business.

This creative exercise is going to show you how to open your creative energy by taking productive breaks in your day.

Almost every productivity article will tell you that you need to add in time to take productive breaks during your day. And when you read those words, you say, "I know about that, let me just finish with this client work or input this stack of data into a spreadsheet and I'll take some kind of break."

But we never do take that much needed break.

As weird as this is going to sound, the reason you don't take a productive break is because you really don't know what to do. Taking a break or – as I like to call it daydreaming – requires discipline and a bit of planning on your part to do it.

Creative Tools needed:
- Notebook and your favorite pen
- Your imagination
- Quiet place outside for 30 minutes

With your shoes on or off, step outside.

Take a walk, sit on the porch or just go outside in your front yard.

Whatever you do, make sure to leave your cell phone in your pocket. Disconnect from everything and do NOT take it out except to check the time.

Now, look up at the sky and daydream. Let your mind wander past those thoughts telling you that this is a strange way to spend 30 minutes.

Watch the clouds and see what shapes you can imagine. Or if it's a stormy day, look at the colors you see in the sky. How many different colors are in the clouds?

Then move your view to the landscape around you. Notice the trees, bushes, flowers, fences, whatever is in your immediate area. Don't think about how you need to mow the grass or fix that hole in the fence. Just notice the colors and shapes and sizes of everything around you.

After 30 minutes of spending time with your daydreams, go inside, grab your favorite pen and a piece of paper to draw something that you saw during your time outside.

Don't worry if your picture looks like something a kindergartener would draw. It's not about being perfect. It's about creating for the pure sake of spending time creating.

Afterwards, make some time to do a Get Out of Your Box check-in with your creative energy.

Questions to use after the creative exercises:

1. What did I learn about myself after doing the Daydream exercise?

_____

_____

_____

_____

_____

2. What did it show me about what happens with my thoughts when I'm adding more creative energy in my life?

_____

_____

_____

_____

_____

3. I am excited about _____

4. I'm proud that I did _____

5. What did you create after doing the creative exercise?

_____

_____

_____

_____

_____

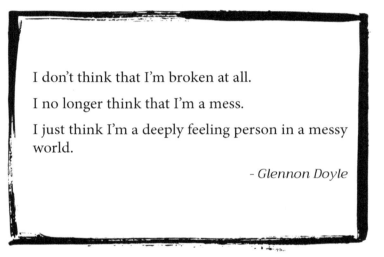

I don't think that I'm broken at all.

I no longer think that I'm a mess.

I just think I'm a deeply feeling person in a messy world.

- Glennon Doyle

CHAPTER FIVE

The Creative Process Can Get Messy

Given the ever-changing world, while making your PIVOT, it should come as no surprise that the internal work you'll find yourself diving into can get messy.

This messiness you'll experience can take the form of solving a problem in a new way, using an innovative idea to promote a new business or the simple act of doing something completely different when responding to an outside shift within your personal life.

In this part of the **Creative Insight Process**, I want you to start thinking about how you're going to increase the amount of time you spend every week living a creative lifestyle. Because when you open your world to your creative energy, you'll expand your thoughts and learn how to take more risks expressing your authenticity.

Remember that expanding your time being creative isn't about being an artist!

It's about finding time in your day to feel happy being in your creative energy.

Think about this part of the process and ask yourself, when was the last time you took pictures for fun or to make a family album? Why do all those square spaces on Instagram have to be about your latest product or a selfie sharing how hard your day was?

What would happen if you spent a week posting images that were just plain fun on Instagram? Making the time to add in something silly to your Instagram feed is a quick way to start increasing moments of pure daily enjoyment from creating rather than focusing on where you are in your life.

One of the best ways to incorporate the **Creative Insight Process** into your world is to move from researching all the information about your problems to finding the right questions to use to solve them.

Stop using research as an excuse to remain stuck. Shift gears and become a Creative Problem Finder.

How do you find the right problems to solve?

During the 1960s, two University of Chicago social scientists began studying creativity. One of their experiments sent them to the School of Art Institute of Chicago to work with fourth-year art students.

The scientists brought the art students into a studio with two large tables in the center. One of the tables was empty and the other table held several objects. The objects ranged from the ordinary, like a book, to the unique, like feathers, that the school used for their drawing classes.

The art students were asked to choose one or more of the objects and arrange a still life display on the empty table. Then they were instructed to create a drawing of the still life objects they'd chosen.

The scientists watched the artists and noted the students fell into two distinct categories: One group approached the project by quickly reviewing the still life objects and began their drawings within minutes of the assignment.

The other group spent their time examining the objects; some artists even moved them into different positions, rearranging the items several times before they started to draw the still life display.

The scientists noted the first group was trying to SOLVE the problem of "What can I use to create a good drawing?"

The second, more intentional, group was trying to FIND a problem and asked themselves, "What kind of drawing do I want to create?"

Afterwards, they conducted a mini art show with all the students' drawings. A panel of art experts at the college found that the problem finders' drawings were far more creative than the problem solvers' artwork.

If we take the results of this experiment and apply them to making your PIVOT, it comes down to taking this process beyond the level of being a problem solver.

You'll need to learn how to be a problem finder by doing the work to uncover possibilities about how to make the change in your life that you're seeking.

The idea is to spend more time understanding that you're looking for solutions to your questions rather than fixing a problem.

Why Creativity is your best problem-finding tool

Before I discovered the **Creative Insight Process**, when there was a problem with something in my world, I would jump right into looking for a solution.

I know that I'm not the only one who does this. Consider what happened to Jennifer, one of my social media consulting clients before she worked with me on her marketing strategy for her new business.

Jennifer decided she was going to figure this social media stuff out.

She ran a Google search to see what advice she could find. She searched for tips and hacks, found a 10-step checklist, registered for a free webinar - anything to help her fix her problem.

She found blog posts that made her think that she was creating social posts the wrong way. And then to add to her confusion, someone told her she was using the wrong social sites to find qualified customers to grow her business.

Jennifer pushed forward with their advice and a few weeks later, she was right back where she started.

She fell into this unrelenting pattern of finding more answers and trying out one thing after another until she would shrug her shoulders and think, "Well, that didn't work either. What's next?"

It's easy to just keep following this cycle of research, until you stop long enough to consider what the problem really is. Do you really want a real solution to your problem, or can you honestly admit that you're doing all these steps for the pure sake of saying that it's fixed?

When you find yourself in this place, you have gone into the research version of autopilot. Your quest leads you to keep searching for answers, listening to one more person on YouTube telling you what they think you want to hear.

To stop this endless loop of trying to fix the problem, I want to bring in the next piece of this process with something called Creative Problem Solving.

This part of the **Creative Insight Process** focuses more on using your imagination to find solutions to your questions. Becoming a creative problem solver is going to disrupt the 'everyone-says-to-do-it-this-way-pattern' and gives you a fresh perspective about how you can PIVOT most effectively.

Your new Creative Problem-Solving skills can be learned by following some steps to give you a framework to uncover new innovative ideas that will lead you to the answers that you're seeking:

1. **Start by asking your problems as open-ended questions.**

   Be curious about seeking out new options as the answers to your problems by using open-ended questions that have multiple possibilities. Close-ended questions where you'll land with a 'yes' or a 'no' will only provide you with limited options when what you really need to do is challenge your assumptions.

   Try starting your questions with words like Why, What If, How Could I and Where Else and see where that path takes you.

2. **Suspend your judgement.**

   When it comes to the Creative Problem-Solving process, making a quick judgement when you get an idea { like oh that's not me, I can't do that kind of thing! } will shut it down completely before you've had time to truly flesh it out.

   Your initial ideas will come in raw first draft form. These ideas need time to grow and develop into what could possibly be the biggest game changer in your life.

Don't allow your fears or anxiety about your initial idea to make it invalid. Ask yourself why did this even pop into my head? Is there a piece of this idea that I could turn into an opportunity for my PIVOT?

Catch yourself when you immediately look for ways to find fault with your idea.

What would happen if you tried out just one piece of the idea, one step or spent 15 minutes testing out how that app worked on your phone?

Remind yourself that this thought came to you for a reason. What's the message this thought is trying to send you about what you should be doing?

3. **Add these two words to your internal conversation: Yes, and**

   Even though the use of the words 'Yes, and' has its foundations in improvisational { improve } comedy, it's an incredible technique to start developing your Creative Problem-Solving process.

   The improv technique works like this: no matter what comes up in your internal conversation, respond with the words 'Yes, and' instead of starting your response with the word 'but.'

   When you bring the word 'but' into the conversation, you immediately start to negate your idea and everything that came before it. No matter what you're feeling inside about your idea, your job is to keep saying the words 'Yes, and' to allow yourself to continue exploring all the opportunities and paths to uncover your answer.

   Let's use our friend Carol the Empty Nester who likes to bake cakes as an example of how this works. As she starts to develop the idea of selling her cakes to the art boutique shop, it would have been easy for her thoughts to go to "sure you like to bake but you've never had a job or run a small business" or she could say, "I know that kids at school liked your cakes but they're kids; no one will want to buy something that they can make themselves."

   Can you see how easy it would be for Carol to discourage herself from starting her new cake selling business if she kept saying 'but' to herself?

   What would happen if Carol started using the words 'Yes, and?' Let's look at a conversation that she could have with herself in her kitchen:

   "What can I do to sell my cakes to that cute little store downtown? I've got this great chocolate cake recipe ... **Yes, and** I've made cupcakes with it for the kids at my son's school."

"I've never been a business owner; I don't even know where to start ... **Yes, and** I can always talk to my husband to get his help. He's been working at an investment company, he's probably full of suggestions."

"What if none of my cakes sell at the downtown shop? **Yes, and** I'll be okay. I'll be proud of myself for even taking the cakes down to the manager and trying something new."

Read those sentences out loud to yourself and see how it feels to say the words 'Yes, and' instead of using the word 'but' to tell yourself why something isn't going to work.

Your success with making your PIVOT is directly connected to your ability to creatively solve where you are so you can get to where you want to be. And one of the best tools that you can use to get you there is your ability to use the Creative Problem-Solving steps to become a problem finder in your PIVOT process.

For you to connect this problem solving work with your creative energy, you need to do two things:

1. Consistent repetition and reinforcement

2. Ability to disrupt the pattern { we'll get into this more in the next chapter }

You'll need to consistently spend time being creative to make a change with your pattern { your habits } to eventually make that big PIVOT.

Your Creative Problem-Solving process isn't going to give you a quick fix to suddenly find relief from your anxiety or fears so you can make a new change in your path. Just know that the constant use of this process will help you move through it with less pain and more joy.

What do I mean by consistent repetition and reinforcement?

I want you to think about how you can do something creative once a day for 30 days. And on the days that you're not doing a creative thing, spend about 15 minutes thinking about what you need to do to prepare for that week's creative thing.

Let's say that you've decided you want to spend your creative energy gardening every Saturday morning, while everyone's still asleep so you can spend that time in peace outside.

If you're going to be in the garden every Saturday morning, for the rest of that week, you'll think about what you need to get from the garden store, when you'll drive down to the store and then you'll spend the rest of your time during the week planning out what you'll plant and where.

The creative activity will happen on Saturday but Monday through Friday, you'll be spending time in your creative energy getting yourself ready to get your hands dirty. Then on Sunday, you'll sit in your garden to look at the work you've done and start to think about the next thing you will plant or buy to add to your space.

Consistently engaging with your creative project during the week will start to refocus your thoughts and train your brain to create new pathways. The reinforcement of thinking about your creative project will allow you to bring in more positive peptides into your brain and help you to move past the anxiety and worry and into those feelings of joy.

I know you're all in with this idea but come on, 30 days? You want me to do this every day for 30 days? And I'm like yeah - yeah, I do want you to do this for 30 days.

I want you to think about building up your creative energy muscle like you were a professional bodybuilder training for an event.

Do you think that guy is in incredible shape because he does a few reps with a small weight once every other week? Nope. He does a workout every day. Every day he's in that gym working through constant repetition of his muscles and retraining his body to be stronger so he can lift more weights.

I want you to think of this process as training your mind to bring creative energy into your daily thoughts.

And because you're a creative bodybuilder, you're not going to do this for two weeks and stop and be like, "I knew this didn't work." That's not how you're going to win the bodybuilding competition and get the big prize.

Accept that you won't be perfect when you start. Your brain isn't used to these thoughts so for you to see the results you want; you'll need to push through your excuses and learn how to disrupt your brain's usual pattern of worry and fears.

To be consistent, you'll need to have a plan in place to keep you on track with this process to start to train your brain and body.

You can set a timer on your phone every day if you need to remind yourself to spend time in your creative energy space. You can set up a habit tracker app to remind yourself to think about your creative project, whatever works for you, do it.

A painful lesson of retraining

I had no reason to be hospitalized for 17 years until November 2020.

The last time I had seen the inside of a hospital room was when I gave birth to my son Jake. All that changed that day in November when I spent the weekend in the Emergency Room.

No - I didn't have COVID nor did anyone else in my life. I'm thankful that's not the reason I was a frequent visitor to the ER that month.

I was bitten by a spider.

Not just any kind of spider but a poisonous one. And to make this worse, that spider didn't just bite me - I sat on it. There was a painful bite in a weird awkward place on the back of my thigh, making it hard to sit still for long periods of time.

I was secretly hoping that I would wake up with some kind of superpower. Isn't that what happened to Spiderman? He got bitten by a spider and got those web things in his hands and super strength.

So far, no superpowers have revealed themselves. All I have is a weird discolored spot on the back of my leg where the bite healed.

It was a painful learning lesson, but it taught me a few things about how to retrain my body - and to make sure that you look at the chair before you sit down.

I used to think that I was invincible, and I could push through anything. But that experience caught me completely off guard. I had to figure out how I was going to heal from the hole in the back of my leg.

I'm really into finding time in my week to go walking anywhere for three to five miles for each walk. Somedays, I walk my dog downtown by the lake, or

I'll drive to the other end of town to walk by the river to watch the boats come in. I make time for these walks not just for my physical health but my mental health as well.

Being outside my house and in nature gives me time to clear my head and move my body off the couch.

As I started to heal from the spider bite, it was hard for me to go on a long walk.

I couldn't make it around the lake without having to slow down and take a break. It was frustrating not being able to move at my usual speedy pace, but my leg had a hole from where they cut the spider poison out and I could feel the bandages pulling causing me extra pain if I moved too fast or went too far.

It would have been easy for me to take a break from my weekly walks and claim that I needed time to heal. But that's not how I roll. I knew I needed to retrain my body to walk again.

I needed to put a plan in place. At first, I went smaller distances and just figured out how to limp my way through on my bad leg.

But I kept on going and adding in extra daily walks with my dog just to keep my body moving towards healing. After the first month, the limping stopped and by the second month, I wasn't back to my speedy pace but at least, I was back to my usual distance of walking at least three miles.

Trust me when I say that I understand what you're feeling desiring to make that big PIVOT in your life. And I can tell you from my experience that when you keep at it, when you build on your progress, you will see the shifts happening within your mind and your body.

Always keep your head up, especially when you're beginning to climb up the hill, even if you have a pain in the back of your leg that's throbbing and telling you to stop. Don't let your excuses or the pain of your spider bite stop you from being consistent with your plan.

You must believe in yourself and trust that things will move into the direction that you're desiring.

So many things in life are not worth getting worked up over and causing you to stop your momentum. I admit that I'm not always particularly good at recognizing that, but I can assure you that this will change for you when you become consistent with spending your time in your creative energy.

GET OUT OF YOUR BOX CREATIVE EXERCISE #4: BRICK VS BLANKET

This creative exercise is part of a divergence test that measures how you use your imagination. This test is set up to see how far your mind can reach into different directions.

Know that there is no single right answer. Your goal with this exercise is to go for QUANTITY while not being concerned about the QUALITY of your answers.

Creative Tools needed:
- Notebook and your favorite pen OR a Word document
- Your imagination
- A timer on your phone or something in your home
- Quiet place for 10 minutes

Set your timer for five minutes and write/type out as many different uses that you can think of for **a brick**.

There is no right or wrong answer, just write what comes to your mind.

I know that the first few minutes will go quickly as you write things like a brick can be used to build houses, as a doorstop and a weight in the wind. Afterwards you may feel like you're out of answers but keep pushing yourself for the full five minutes.

Then set your timer for another 5 minutes and write/type out as many different uses that you can think of **a blanket**.

I'll get you started with the blanket - to keep warm on a bed, as a tent, as a makeshift hammock in the backyard. Again, I encourage you to keep pushing on with your answers for the full five minutes.

Keep using your imagination, even if it sounds silly, until you've come up with as many answers as you can for both the brick and the blanket. You'll find that the ones at the end of this exercise will be completely out of the box for how to use these two objects but that means that you're digging deep into your imagination.

Opening up your imagination with this exercise will generate your creative energy. I encourage you to go with it after your 10 minutes are up. Dig around your house and see what you have available to make something that brings you joy.

Remember all those things you made when you were in grade school from stuff you found around your house? Go find some fun items and see what you can make with them.

Remember, it's not about being perfect. It's about creating for the pure sake of spending time creating.

After you're finished with your home-made creation, do the next Get Out of Your Box check-in to see where you are in the creativity process.

Questions to use after the creative exercises:

1. What did I learn about myself after doing the Brick vs Blanket exercise?

   _____

   _____

   _____

   _____

2. What did it show me about what happens with my thoughts when I'm adding more creative energy in my life?

   _____

   _____

   _____

   _____

3. I am excited about _____

4. I'm proud that I did _____

5. What did you create after doing the creative exercise? Did you create something else other than your home-made art project?

   _____

   _____

   _____

   _____

The creative process is not like a situation where you get struck by a single lightning bolt. You have ongoing discoveries, and there's ongoing creative revelations. Yes, it's really helpful to be marching toward a specific destination, but, along the way, you must allow yourself room for your ideas to blossom, take root, and grow.

- Carlton Cuse

CHAPTER SIX

How to Disrupt the Pattern

By now you understand that you need to retrain your brain and body to make the big shift in your life. I gave you some steps on how you can move through this process with consistent reinforcement but what was that thing about disrupting the pattern?

When you first started learning about this process, I shared with you that when you decide to make a change in your life, you have two choices. You can go into autopilot and do the same thing you always do. Or you can disrupt your patterns by thinking differently within your prefrontal cortex.

I shared with you what happened to me when I made the choice to disrupt my own way of thinking when COVID hit my business and instead of stew in worry, I started to paint.

Think of your patterns like this - almost everything that you do in your life is something that you developed from habit, from where you go to walk your dog to how you make coffee in the morning. There was a good reason why you started doing these steps in this specific pattern but eventually, you stopped asking yourself why and you just did it.

A pattern is your learned response to a stimulus. That stimulus can be anything from a person, a smell, taste or even a noise. No matter what the stimulus is, your brain and body react the same way; like the way you might hit the snooze button three times when your alarm goes off in the morning.

We've all been raised with a series of patterns.

As kids, we had bedtime routines and actions that we did every day at school. As adults, we've shifted our desire for patterns into the way that you drive the same route to work every day or go down the same aisles at the same grocery store every week.

Your brain loves it when you can develop a pattern like this. It makes you feel safe and like there's order to your world.

Patterns aren't only in your physical world. Your patterns can also include your beliefs, thoughts, and feelings. And while you can't always control the stimulus around yourself, you can control the way you respond.

And since your brain is programmed to feel safe in these patterns that you created, this is one of the main reasons why it feels so hard to make a change. Your brain wants to feel the comfort of the patterns and any resistance can cause you to react physically - like when you have the feeling of butterflies in your stomach.

The first step to move out of autopilot is to reflect on your day and think about the actions that you do every day. Notice the patterns of actions that you're doing without even realizing why or how you're getting them done. That moment of consciousness about the actions you're doing will be a huge step forward in learning how to disrupt your patterns.

Know going into this part of the **Creative Insight Process** that your body will physically resist the changes you're trying to make. You're going to get uncomfortable but know these feelings are temporary.

Like the creative bodybuilder you are, you're going to feel the soreness from lifting that heavy weight. But when you're able to recognize the pattern in your thoughts and feelings that's not working and stops you with all its excuses, you'll be able to choose how to change your thoughts to get you where you want to go.

You've likely heard the expression that "life is 10% of what happens to you and 90% of how you react to it." And if we truly believe that we have control over how we react to something, then it opens us up to more opportunities because you know that you have a choice about how to respond.

Once you can accept that you'll feel discomfort like fear, worry and anxiety, and that you'll come out into a better place afterwards, that's when you start moving through the familiar into thinking differently. Then you're really ready to disrupt these behavioral patterns within your brain's pathways.

One of the best things you can do to start thinking differently and move through your PIVOT is to choose a new set of thoughts to replace the uncomfortable ones. The secret sauce to disrupt your patterns is to move your focus from fighting the old habits of thought into building your new thought pathways.

As you've already learned, your brain is hardwired with the peptides to keep you doing the same thing, thinking the same thoughts - even the bad ones! - because your body will always go back to its comfort box.

When you make a conscious effort to override those neural pathways, you'll find yourself going in an opposite direction rather than towards the familiar. The more you disrupt your patterns, the easier it'll be to free yourself of the bad thoughts and move you closer to what you really want to do with your life.

It's like that thing they call the Costanza Rule from the *Seinfeld* show that featured one of the best characters to ever hit sitcom TV - George Costanza.

In the episode called "The Opposite," George finds himself disrupting his patterns. After years of failing at all things in his personal life to the different jobs he has on the show, George has an ah-ha moment: When he follows his instincts to do something it always leads to disastrous outcomes. George comes up with the idea to do the exact opposite of what his gut instinct is telling him to do.

Are we surprised that when George does the opposite of what he would otherwise choose to do, he finds himself on the right side of every decision? In the rest of the episode, we watch George completely disrupt his pattern from what he orders for lunch to how he interacts with his boss at work. His usual routine of finding things that go against him turns into the unfamiliar feeling of success.

For this process to work for you, I strongly suggest that you be open to following George Constanza's way of thinking. As you continue your journey sorting through how you're going to move forward with your PIVOT, recognize that there will be times when the best action you can take is the exact opposite of the one that you always choose.

It is extremely important to trust your feelings surrounding your choices when you're paying attention to your gut instinct. Don't always look towards the familiar but remain open to new ideas and to the creative energy in your life.

How to harness your Creative Problem-Solving Skills

When it comes to putting your creative problem-solving skills in action, I'm in no way saying that doing the opposite like George Costanza means being hurtful towards anything or anybody.

If your instinct is to respond in a kind and genuine way, going against your gut's internal emotions to being rude and disrespectful is not the path that's going to move you into the right neural pathways to make your PIVOT.

When I say do the opposite like George, I'm referring to going against your autopilot actions.

If when doing one of the creative exercises, an idea comes to you to create a video to teach your potential new customers something to solve a problem, I'm encouraging you to explore this idea. Especially if you're that person who spent ten minutes thinking through how you'll set up your stuff to clearly explain the solution you're going to do in the video - and then you're also that person who spent the next 30 minutes talking yourself out of all the reasons that you're just not one of those people who does videos.

If that amazing idea came to you in the stillness of your creative energy, call on your inner George Costanza and don't let those inner thoughts talk you out of all the reasons that your comfort zone would want you to follow. For you to be open to the innovative ideas to make your shift, you need to learn how to disrupt your habitual patterns.

Being creative is one of the best ways that you'll be able to think differently where you'll come up with fresh ideas that you may not have thought about before.

Here are some ways that you can start to disrupt your patterns using your creative energy:

1. **When you spend more time in your creative space, you'll come up with more original ideas that will get you closer to the best solution that works for you.** With a typical brainstorming technique, you could end up with one or two great ideas. But with such a small list of options, you'll limit yourself. And there's a good chance that you'll spend more time trying to figure out how to fit your plan into those limited options rather than seeing that it's not working for your desired goal.

   Creative problem-solving allows you to come up with more than a couple of options. When you work the creative problem-solving process, you'll uncover so many more options that you could try. Granted not all these ideas will work for what you're trying to shift in your life but one or two them combined could be more in line with what's going to work for where you're trying to go.

2. **There's no way to force your creative energy to work.** Your most amazing ideas will come to you as a creative breakthrough and will happen spontaneously as you're engaging your creative actions.

   The more you engage in your creative activities like gardening, cooking, painting, or taking your dog to a new park by a lake, the more you'll allow your brain to stay open to the new thoughts. The more you remove yourself from living on autopilot and find time to disrupt your habits, the more often you'll experience a creative breakthrough.

3. **Give yourself as much time as you can.** I get it; sometimes you don't have a lot of time and you need to act immediately. But for most of the things you'll be working through, you have all the time you want. It's your life and your choices that you're sorting through.

   Give yourself all the days that you can to think through your ideas and options. The more time you have and the less pressure you put on yourself, the greater the chance of uncovering the optimal solution for your next step forward.

   Notice I said DAYS not weeks or worse, years. This step isn't a reason for you to procrastinate making the next step because you're giving yourself the space to think it through. Take the time you need but don't give yourself permission to not decide on your next step.

4. **Practice being persistent.** Practicing persistence requires you to stay focused on your goal even when life becomes challenging. Making a big PIVOT isn't going to happen overnight just like winning the lottery isn't suddenly going to make you a financial investment genius.

You need time to research information, time to learn new technology and time to make new connections who can help you to your goal. Persistence means accepting that your progress will take time, but it also requires you to be consistent with the daily actions to keep training your brain and body to move into the new solutions you're seeking.

One of the best ways to practice being persistent is to learn how to do something called 'stacking your habits' from Author James Clear's book *Atomic Habits.*

This productivity step will help you turn a behavior into a habit with something called a trigger.

A trigger is an action that you're already doing. It's something that's already a part of your day like checking your email at a certain time of day.

You can take one of your current habits that you've built into your day and use that as a trigger for your new action item.

Let's say you want to grow your side business and increase the amount of money you're making. To build your business, you've decided to use Facebook to connect with more customers. You already have a habit of logging into Facebook every day at lunchtime to check what's going on with your Facebook friends and your family.

If your goal is to grow your customers by increasing your engagement in the Facebook Group you manage, then logging into your Facebook app becomes your trigger.

You log into Facebook, check what's going on with your friends { your trigger } and then head over to your Facebook Group for 20 minutes to spend time posting and commenting on your members' posts { your new habit }.

When starting out with this new process, your existing habit acts as a trigger until one day, logging into Facebook becomes 15 minutes checking in with your family and then another 15 minutes for Facebook Groups. It becomes second nature to do these two things in a row.

Once you've gotten into a routine to stack these two social media habits, you can add in a third.

Maybe another goal is to increase your connections by commenting in other Facebook Groups. Now when you log into Facebook, you've got a stack of three habits – checking on your family and friends, posting in the Facebook Group you manage and then commenting in two other Facebook Groups.

Each Facebook habit acts as a trigger to do the next one until it becomes part of your daily or weekly routine to do all three of habits together to grow your Facebook presence.

Think about the new habits you want to bring into your life to make your PIVOT. See how you can set up one action as the trigger and which other steps you'll bring in to stack your habits to move you closer to your goals.

GET OUT OF YOUR BOX CREATIVE EXERCISE #5: A TITLE IN EIGHT WORDS

In your last creative exercise, you're going to push yourself and disrupt the patterns in your thoughts by creating a headline or story title that comes with a backstory or something that creates a curiosity to know more.

The fun part about this exercise - you are limited to only eight words for each title.

The idea came from the famous Hemingway title that he did in six words:

"For Sale: Baby Shoes. Never Worn."

{ You can read more about the history of this title by running a search on Hemingway in Wikipedia. }

Creative Tools needed:
- Notebook and your favorite pen OR a Word document
- Your imagination
- Quiet place for 15 minutes

This exercise focuses on how you can push your imagination to generate curiosity and to make the reader want to know more. This creative exercise is going to be harder than you think but keep pushing yourself to disrupt your usual answers and to think out of the box.

A good tip is to use words that you normally don't use together. You can write as many titles as you want in your 15-minute timeframe but just make sure that your title or headline makes someone want to know the rest of the story.

Here are a few examples.

Title: My trip to Europe. Cancel or go alone?

Curiosity: Why am I going to Europe? What happened to the person I was going on the trip with?

Title: Looking to buy a new home. Discretion required.

Curiosity: Why would you need discretion when you're buying a new home? What happened to make you want to move and buy another house?

If you feel like you want to keep going after your 15-minutes are up, get out another piece of paper or open a new Word document. Take each of your titles and write out a backstory that answers your curiosity questions.

It can be as long or short as you like, just keep writing until you feel you've completed the whole story.

After you've completed this creative exercise, answer the questions below to do a Get Out of Your Box check-in with where you are in the creativity process.

Questions to use after the creative exercises:

1. What did I learn about myself after doing the A Title in Eight Words exercise?

_____

_____

_____

2. What did it show me about what happens with my thoughts when I'm adding more creative energy in my life?

_____

_____

_____

3. I am excited about _____

4. I'm proud that I did _____

5. What did you create after doing the creative exercise? Did you write out the backstory to the titles you came up with?

_____

_____

_____

CONCLUSION

Come On, Get Happy

You made it through this book, which can only mean one thing - you're ready to do something different, ready to think differently and you've become more aware of the things that you'll be doing to make that big PIVOT in your life.

It's time to put this book down and start taking action to find more time in your world to be happy:

1. **Spend more time paying attention to when your thoughts create a physical reaction in your body.** Think about what's happening in your emotional brain. Have you trained your body for the good feeling peptides or to crave more of the anxious stressful peptides? Remember that the body doesn't know the difference between the good feelings and the bad ones. Notice when your body is telling you that something is off and adjust your thoughts to send a bigger rush of joyful thoughts into your body.

2. **Start thinking big and dig into your imagination.** Challenge your preconceived thoughts about how something is supposed to look, see or feel. Open your mind to the silly and out-of-the-box ideas by starting your internal conversations with phrases like 'What if?" and 'How could I?'

3. **Tap into the Creative Insight Process.** How can you add creative energy into your week? Bonus points for finding time to bring creative ideas into your day like taking a walk in a different direction around the neighborhood. Create new habits in your life where you replace your autopilot actions into something that will bring more opportunities to feel good.

4. **Roll up your sleeves and get ready to make a mess.** When you feel yourself getting stuck, go back through the Creative Problem-Solving steps like asking open-ended questions, suspending your judgement about the ideas that come up and then 'Yes, And' that thing until you land on your next path to keep moving forward.

5. **It works when you work it.** Build up your creative muscles by putting a plan in place to be consistent with the process. Accept that there will be days when you're just not all that into it but do it anyway. The more you're consistent with living in your creative energy, the more you'll retrain your brain and body to spend more time in the space where you'll be open to new opportunities. And you'll know when you've hit that place when your body craves being creative more than it wants to spend time living in a place of worry.

6. **Accept that you're going to get uncomfortable and you may feel physical discomfort when you start to disrupt your patterns.** Don't let the brain make excuses for you to stop. Remember this feeling is only temporary until your choices and thoughts become a new habit. Practice looking for ways that you can create a positive trigger to help you stay focused on your goals.

Getting closer to your goals

Some days it feels like the hours just fly by and you ask yourself, "What just happened? Did I get anything done to keep me moving towars my goals? Was I even productive?"

I admit, I've had days when my answer to those questions was NO. And that kinda sucks.

I know that it happens to all of us. Then we justify the day by telling ourselves – not every day can be a winner. Hey, I showed up and turned on my laptop, right?

Well, yeah ... but is that getting you closer to your goals? Is this going to help you make that big PIVOT in your life? Probably not.

I know this game.

I know this game we play all too well. And I played it with all the grace and style of someone who found herself stuck in the same place every year.

I'd do my year in review and wonder how I started January being proactive with so much enthusiasm and end it in December, feeling like I'm just reacting to what was going on outside of me.

But your year-end review isn't going to be a wrap up of what you've done to react to what's going on around you. It's going to be different for you when you do the work of adding the **Creative Insight Process** into your life.

This will be your time to make that big leap.

Make a commitment to yourself that things are going to change and when you hit December, you aren't going to be scratching your head, wondering what happened.

Because now you know what you need to do to make things happen. And now you've learned one big thing:

We all have the same 24 hours in a day. It's how we choose to use them that makes the difference.

How will you choose to show up to make a difference?

You already have the answers within you about how to show up and really make that PIVOT you've been thinking about. You just need the creative tools to help you move your ideas from just swirling around in your head to developing a plan with action steps to help you show up in your new life.

Before I started doing the process that I've shared with you, I was living in a space where I was constantly responding to what was happening outside of me.

I had my plans. I had my strategy to build my business. I had my list of all the goals I wanted to achieve ... but what would happen? Somewhere along the way, I got off track.

I would spend way too much time in my head thinking about how "I can't do this thing" or "How am I going to do that?" Quite honestly - most of the reasons that you don't push through to the next level is because you get caught up in all those negative thoughts swirling around in your head.

You stop your progress because somehow, you've convinced yourself that this thing that you want is just not possible. You create constraints related to your budget, time and whether you even have the skills to make it happen.

I speak from personal experience because I've spent a lot of years convincing myself that this was just the way it's gotta be.

But when I worked through the interactive workbooks in the **Create Your Business** subscription box program, I spent more time in the creative right-brain side of my world. Those constraints I put on myself started to fall away.

I learned that to create what I wanted for my business and my personal life, I needed to stop what I had always done and do something to help me think differently.

The year 2020 gave me the time to take a deep pause and to take a look at the work I was doing to build my business. Everything changed for me when I realized that I wasn't going to find success because of the perfect to-do list or if I was using the right social media app.

Success wasn't going to happen to me. It was going to happen because of me.

Using my right-brain thinking put me in a place where I could come up with unique solutions to turn my ideas into an income-producing business.

If you're ready to make a change and see how this process can apply to your small business, I want to invite you to visit my website for more resources, tools and to try out the **Create Your Business** subscription box program. It's part interactive workbook with creative exercises { like the ones you experienced in this book } that comes to your inbox and part creative tools that get delivered to your doorstep.

Your monthly **Create Your Business** box is filled with art supplies to help you welcome fresh ideas to develop your marketing strategy to reach more qualified customers.

If you're ready to see how the **Creative Insight Process** can help you develop marketing messages to help you build your business, subscribe to the **Create Your Business** program: https://createyourbiz.net/

Are you ready to do this?

I realized that no one is immune from experiencing any kind of adversity. That's just the nature of what it's like to be a human in this world.

What really counts is how you decide to manage your choices.

I've given you a new pathway to find your way through. I've given you the tools to move past your fear and to shift your thoughts into a different place where you can ride the wave or make a hard turn into another direction.

As you continue your journey, I want you to believe that your big goals will come true. Once you genuinely believe in all the beauty that you are, your true path will reveal itself.

To quote Author Henry Miller, "The moment one gives close attention to anything, even a blade of grass, it becomes a mysterious, awesome, indescribably magnificent world in itself."

You are magnificent my friend. You are meant to see your dreams come true.

And let me be the first to say, I'm proud of you.

About the Author

My name is Penney Fox. I'm more than just a social media consultant – I'm a Social Media Productivity Coach.

I own a social media consulting company that's NOT like a typical social marketing agency. I'm here to teach you practical productivity steps to help you grow your online presence to connect you with more qualified people who want to buy your services, your products or online coaching programs.

I've been running my own business since 1999 so I understand the daily struggle to grow your business while still finding time for something that at least resembles a personal life.

In 2019, I developed the Create Your Business hybrid subscription box program. It's like self-coaching in a box where every month, you'll get an interactive workbook sent to your inbox and creative tools that show up at your doorstep to help you develop your marketing messages to reach more customers online.

The Create Your Business programs can be found at CreateYourBiz.net and her book I Just Did a Thing - A Creative Approach to Pivoting and Designing Revolutionary Changes in Life and Business can be found on the same site as well as ordered from Amazon.

Printed in Great Britain
by Amazon

18287353R00041